"Soft good cat cat."
—Koko

One-year-old Koko.

preface

Other animals are capable of telling us about themselves—if we can find the right way to ask them.

I met Koko in 1972 at the San Francisco Zoo when she was a year old. Six months earlier, Koko had become seriously ill and was removed from her gorilla group. She had recovered and was being cared for by volunteers in the Zoo nursery.

A lecture in 1971 about a chimpanzee who learned how to communicate in American Sign Language—ASL for short—impressed me. As a graduate school student studying developmental

In memory of All Ball.

Copyright © 1985/2009 by The Gorilla Foundation
The Gorilla Foundation/National Geographic Society
All rights reserved. Published by The Gorilla Foundation
Photographs copyright © by Ronald Cohn/ The Gorilla Foundation
Art direction JohnPaul Slater

Library of Congress Cataloging in Publication Data
Patterson, Francine,
Koko's kitten.
Summary: The real life experience of Koko, a gorilla
in California who uses sign language, with a young kitten
whom she loved and grieved over when it died.
1. Koko (Gorilla)—Juvenile literature. 2. Kittens—
Juvenile literature. [1. Koko (Gorilla) 2. Gorillas.
3. Cats. 4. Human–animal communication] I. Title.
QL737.P96P38 1985 599.88'46 85–2311
ISBN 978-0-615-24698-7

12 11 10 9 8 7   5/9

Printed in the U.S.A.   37

Koko's Kitten

by Dr. Francine "Penny" Patterson

photographs by Dr. Ronald H. Cohn

The Gorilla Foundation
koko.org

psychology, I wanted to do that kind of work, too.

So I asked the zoo director for permission to care for, and work with, Koko. When I told him I was willing to spend four or five years with her, he gave his consent. It was the first time a study of language abilities had been attempted with a gorilla.

The project that began in 1972 has become my life's work—and Koko's, too. Today Koko knows over one thousand signs and comprehends over 2,000 words of spoken English. She uses signs to name things in her environment, ask questions, tell how she feels, and title her drawings and paintings. Koko is able to communicate her opinions, and has a strong sense of who she is. In fact, when I asked Koko whether she was an animal or a person, she replied, "Fine person gorilla."

There were many times that Koko surprised, enlightened and inspired me, but nothing prepared me for how Koko reacted when a small, grey, tailless kitten came to live with us.

This is the story of Koko and her kitten, All Ball. It is a story in which a gorilla tells us about herself in a language that expresses love, anger, sorrow and joy—and in the process, inspires a newfound respect for all creatures.

Koko signs "cat."

Koko's full name is Hanabi-ko, which is Japanese for Fireworks Child. She was born on the Fourth of July. Every year, I have a party for Koko with cake, sparkling apple cider, and lots of presents.

Koko knows what birthdays are. When asked what she does on her birthday, Koko answered, "Eat, drink, (get) old."

Three days before Koko's party, I said, "I'm going shopping today. What do you want for your birthday?"

"Cereal there. Good there drink," Koko signed.

"But what presents do you want? I asked.

"Cat," answered Koko.

Later, she repeated, "Cat, cat, cat."

"Sleep."
Koko and Penny.

Koko signs "mad."

I wasn't surprised that Koko asked for a cat. I have been reading to Koko for many years and two of her favorite stories have been "Puss in Boots" and "The Three Little Kittens."

Koko gets very involved in stories I read her. When reading the story of the three little kittens who lose their mittens, Koko sees that their mother is angry and that the kittens are crying.

"Mad," Koko signs.

Koko loves picture books. Gorilla books are her favorites. Cat books are next. She likes to go off on her own with a book to study the pictures and sign to herself.

On her birthday, I gave Koko the usual assortment of presents— apple juice, some special fruits and nuts, and a baby doll. I didn't want to give Koko a stuffed toy cat because I knew she'd eventually destroy it.

The only durable toy cat I could find was in a mail order catalogue and I ordered it right away. It was made of cement and covered with vinyl and black velvet. I chose it because it looked real and it was sturdy—gorilla-proof. The toy cat didn't arrive in time for Koko's birthday, so I decided to save it for Christmas.

In December, I made a list for Koko. I drew about twenty pictures—fruits, vegetables, nuts, dolls, combs, and blankets. Every year, Koko gets a stocking and lots of presents. She loves Christmas.

"What do you want for Christmas?" I asked as I showed Koko the pictures. Koko carefully studied the booklet. Then she pointed to a doll, nuts—and a cat.

I bought Koko some nuts and a new doll. I wrapped the toy cat and put it with the rest of her presents.

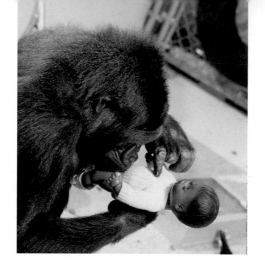

On Christmas morning, Koko ate her cereal and opened her stocking. It was filled with nuts. Koko threw the nuts aside and went to her next present.

Koko unwrapped a doll.

"That stink," Koko signed.

Then came the velvet cat.

"That red," she signed.

Koko often uses the word *red* to express anger. Koko was very upset. She started running back and forth, banging on her walls. She was doing display charges past me. They were angry, angry charges.

It is natural for gorillas to display when frightened or in great danger. They run sideways, pound their chests, then go down on all fours, and run back and forth.

But this was Christmas, usually a happy day for Koko, and she was with people she loved.

Later in the day, Barbara, a friend who had known Koko since she was a baby gorilla, arrived.

"That looks like a black cat," Barbara said to Koko. "Would you show it to me?"

Koko did not answer. She pulled a blanket over her head.

"Could I see it?" Barbara asked.

Koko pulled a rag over the toy cat, then tossed it in the air. "Cat that," Koko signed.

"Please let me see it," said Barbara.

Koko gave her a toy dinosaur instead.

I finally understood Koko's strange behavior. She was unhappy with her Christmas present. I had made a mistake. Koko did not want a cement and velvet toy cat. Koko wanted a real cat.

The toy cat.

9

Things don't always happen quickly where we live. Every day is full of its own activities. So it was almost six months later when Karen, one of my assistants, arrived with three kittens. The kittens had been abandoned by their mother and raised by a dog, a Cairn terrier.

Karen showed the kittens to Koko.

"Love that," Koko signed.

As we showed Koko the kittens, she gave each one her blow test. When Koko meets a new friend, she blows in their face. I think she is trying to get a better scent. When she blows at a person, she expects them to blow back. Maybe she expected the kittens to blow back, too.

The first kitten was smoky gray and white. Koko's blow test took him by surprise. The second kitten was a tailless gray tabby. He was also startled by the blow test. The third kitten, a brown tabby, did not react at all.

After the blow test, Koko seemed to have made some judgements about the kittens.

"Which one do you want?" we asked.

"That," signed Koko, pointing to the tailless tabby.

Koko chooses the tabby.

I am not sure why Koko picked the gray tabby as her favorite. I never asked her. Perhaps it was because he didn't have a tail—a gorilla has no tail.

That night, all three kittens went home with Karen. Two days later, the kittens came back for another visit. Koko was happy to see them.

"Visit love tiger cat," Koko signed.

First she picked up the gray and white one. Then Koko took the tailless tabby and carried him on her thigh. After a while, she pushed him up onto the back of her neck.

"Baby," Koko signed.

She cradled the tabby in her legs and examined its paws. Koko squeezed, and the tabby's claws came out.

"Cat do scratch," Koko signed. "Koko love."

" What will you name the kitty?" I asked.

"All Ball," Koko signed.

"Yes," I said, "like a ball, he has no tail."

Ball stayed overnight as a visiting kitten. By the end of the week, Ball was a permanent member of our household.

Koko had her kitten at last.

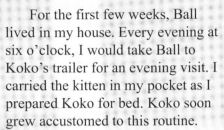

For the first few weeks, Ball lived in my house. Every evening at six o'clock, I would take Ball to Koko's trailer for an evening visit. I carried the kitten in my pocket as I prepared Koko for bed. Koko soon grew accustomed to this routine.

"What happens at night?" I asked.

"All Ball," signed Koko.

"Right," I said. "Ball visits you at night."

When he was older, Ball snuck into Koko's trailer by himself. It worried me in the beginning. I did not know how Koko would treat the kitten unsupervised. As it turned out, Koko was always gentle. Ball was never afraid of her.

Kittens should not be separated from their mothers until they are at least six weeks old. Poor Ball was abandoned by his mother at birth, which might have accounted for some of his behavior.

Ball was an unusual cat. He was very aggressive. He would go up to people and bite them for no reason. He would bite Koko, too.

"Cat bite. Obnoxious," Koko signed, but she never struck back.

Koko did not like to be scratched or bitten, but she loved Ball in spite of his naughty behavior.

"Tell me a story about Ball," I said.

"Koko love Ball," she signed.

Koko signs "love."

Koko tucks Ball in her thigh as she wipes her brow.

Koko carries Ball on her back—just like a gorilla baby.

Koko treated Ball as if he were her baby.

The very first time she picked him up, she tried to tuck him in her thigh. That's where mother gorillas put their infants. Older babies are carried on their mothers' backs. Koko tried this with Ball, too.

Koko was a good gorilla mother. She combed and petted Ball to keep him clean. She also examined his eyes, ears, and mouth to make sure he was healthy. It was Koko who discovered Ball's ear mites.

Ball poses for Koko.

Koko's painting of Ball.

Ball was often a topic of conversation during Koko's lessons.

"Love visit," Koko signed when Ball and I arrived for a morning lesson.

"Ball," I said.

"Trouble," signed Koko. "Love."

Koko seemed to enjoy conversations about her kitten. This dialogue took place between Koko and a research assistant named Janet.

"I'll give you some grapes if you tell me about Ball, the cat," Janet said.

"Soft," Koko signed.

"What kind of animal is he?" Janet asked.

"Cat, cat, cat," Koko answered.

"Do you love Ball?"

"Soft, good cat cat," Koko signed.

In addition to sign language, art is another way I test Koko's perceptions. Ball lay with a green toy on an orange towel. I gave Koko a canvas and some paints and asked her to draw Ball. Koko had ten colors to choose from. First she picked black for Ball's body. Next she picked orange for the towel and green for the toy.

"What about Ball's eyes?" I asked.

Koko picked tan.

Koko loves to play games. Her favorites are "chase," "blow-it," and "tickle."

Koko likes to be tickled, and she thinks that others will like it, too.

"Tickle," Koko signed to Ball when they were lying on the floor together.

Ball was not a good tickler, nor did he like to be tickled. So Koko and I pretended. I tickled Koko while carrying the kitten in my hand. Koko thought this was very funny.

"Chase, blow-it. Enjoy," Koko signed to Ball.

In blow-it, Koko blows as hard as she can into the face of her playmate. It's not hard to understand why this game was not one of Ball's favorites.

Chase is similar to tag. Players run back and forth and chase each other. This is a popular game among gorillas in the wild. But Ball never quite caught on to chase.

Koko did not realize that kittens don't necessarily enjoy gorilla games. Koko did understand that kittens like warmth, affection, and attention. And Koko supplied plenty.

Koko tickles Ball.

On a foggy December morning, one of the assistants told me that Ball had been hit by a car. He had died instantly.

I was shocked and unprepared. I didn't realize how attached I had grown to Ball, and I had no idea how the news would affect Koko. The kitten meant so much to her. He was Koko's baby.

I went to Koko at once. I told her that Ball had been hit by a car; she would not see him again.

Koko did not respond. I thought she didn't understand, so I left the trailer.

Ten minutes later, I heard Koko cry. It was her distress call—a loud, long series of high-pitched hoots.

I cried, too.

Three days later, Koko and I had a conversation about Ball.

"Do you want to talk about your kitty?" I asked.

"Cry," Koko signed.

"Can you tell me more about it?" I asked.

"Blind," she signed.

"We don't see him anymore, do we? What

Koko signs "sad."

happened to your kitty?" I asked.

"Sleep cat," Koko signed.

A few weeks later, Koko saw a picture of a gray tabby who looked very much like Ball. She pointed to the picture and signed, "Cry, sad, frown."

It was an unhappy time.

Koko signs "red."

News of All Ball's death traveled quickly. We received thousands of letters. People of all ages wrote to us and expressed their sympathy. Some sent cards, others sent photographs, and many children created pictures. They all had one message: that Koko should have a new kitten.

As we approached Christmas, I wanted to get Koko a new kitten. I had no idea how difficult that would turn out to be.

On December 20, Barbara asked Koko, "What would you like for Christmas?"

"Cat cat tiger cat," was Koko's reply.

We heard of a Manx who was soon expecting a litter. We waited weeks until we discovered that the cat was just getting fat. Christmas came and went.

Koko's choices

In January I showed Koko a picture of three kittens. One had a long tail, one had a short tail, and one was tailless.

"When you get another kitty, what kind would you like?" I asked.

"That," Koko signed as she pointed to the tailless cat.

"We'll get you a kitty like that," I said. "Is that okay?"

"Good. Nice," Koko answered.

"How do you feel about kitties?" I asked.

"Cat gorilla have visit," she signed. "Koko love."

Koko was ready for a new kitten if only I could find one.

More time went by. I called the Humane Society. They had no kittens at all — let alone a rare, tailless Manx. I called many other places and was disappointed again and again. I was told that not many kittens were born during that time of year.

The worst part of this period was my feeling that I was letting Koko down. I'd watch as someone would ask Koko, "Where's your cat?" And she would look around almost as if she were doing a double take, as if she were looking for Ball.

Then our luck changed. We received a letter from a breeder of Manx cats who wanted to help. He didn't have any kittens then, but he called other Manx breeders nearby until he located a litter of Manx kittens in Southern California. They were just about ready to leave their mother.

We set the date for March 17. The day before, I told Koko she was getting a new kitty — a red kitty. Red is Koko's favorite color. She was very excited.

Then, another delay.

The breeder called. "I'm sorry," he said. "The kitten is not coming today."

Koko was upset. I was disappointed.

"Trouble," she signed.

"We are having trouble getting you a new kitty. We have been trying very hard," I explained.

Finally, on March 24, a red, tiger-striped Manx was brought to our home. Seeing the kitten, Koko purred with pleasure. It was a wonderful moment. She placed him on her chest and petted him.

"Let me hold the kitty," I said.

But Koko would not let go. She kissed and cradled her kitten.

"Baby," she signed.

Koko was happy. Her new kitten had come to stay.

Koko feeds her new kitten, Lipstick.

epilogue

Koko has befriended many in the decades since this award-winning story was first published. She helped teach her adopted younger brother, Michael, to sign, and nurtured him to become a brilliant storyteller and artist. Today another handsome silverback, Ndume, is her constant companion.

Through it all, Gorilla Foundation co-founder Ron Cohn and I have been with Koko every day. We've changed from teachers and foster parents to her closest friends ... and her students.

Today Koko's most important role is as an ambassador for her species. Gorillas have become critically endangered and face many threats to their existence. By distributing *Koko's Kitten* throughout Africa, the Gorilla Foundation is reaching out to touch hearts and change minds, to help the species survive.

To join our family, or get more information, please visit our website, **www.koko.org**. Contributions may be sent to the Gorilla Foundation, P.O. Box 620530, Woodside, CA 94062.

Koko and Michael.